CW01305838

Inspirational Blessings

by

TRACY POSKITT

Order this book online at www.trafford.com
or email orders@trafford.com

Most Trafford titles are also available at major online book retailers.

© Copyright 2011 Tracy Poskitt.

All rights reserved. No part of this publication may be reproduced, stored in a retrieval system, or transmitted, in any form or by any means, electronic, mechanical, photocopying, recording, or otherwise, without the written prior permission of the author.

Printed in the United States of America.

ISBN: 978-1-4269-5185-5 (hc)
ISBN: 978-1-4269-5186-2 (e)

Library of Congress Control Number: 2010918498

Trafford rev. 01/07/2011

www.trafford.com

North America & International
toll-free: 1 888 232 4444 (USA & Canada)
phone: 250 383 6864 ♦ fax: 812 355 4082

I dedicate this book to my late Grandad Earnest who since he passed over to the spirit realms, has worked with me in the role of my Gatekeeper, without him allowing this wisdom to channel through me this book would never have been.

Thanks Tracy

Introduction

This book has been written from spirit, it is blessings from the universe to be shared by all, as a human beings we all need a little message each day to allow ourselves the respect we deserve through our day to day routine in our lives. I am sure that if you hold this book in your heart, you will feel the love that it holds for you. The very fact that this book has been guided to you whether it was a gift or you bought it off a shelf in a book store, it will mean the world to you. It was written with the love of the universe and Tracy Poskitt the channel that was given these blessings. She knew when they were channelled through her that they were for the world. So everyday when you wake up take your blessing and enjoy it with love.

About the Author

The Author of this book is Tracy Poskitt, she is a naturally born light worker and was introduced to spirit at the age of 4, when she was in her bedroom, and Ernest a man with a birth mark came to her and said he would look after her. Tracy shared this with her mum and was told she was dreaming and said there was no such man. Tracy tried to shut this out of her mind, but got more people talking to her. People said that she was daydreaming. Tracy has had many unexplainable experience in her life, as a child she was in the local shop and told them that a ambulance would come to the large lady who lived across the road and take her and that they were waiting for her, sure enough a ambulance did come to the lady, it was too late she had passed over to spirit. Throughout Tracy's childhood as well as her mum taking her to the doctors who gave her pink medicine because she had a nervous condition.

She got bullied from her piers both at home and at school because she was different.

In Tracy's adult life she decided to admit she was different and at the age of 18 went in front of audiences with her spirit work for charity. At the age of 21 Tracy was diagnosed of having multiple sclerosis and along with her medical help also explored Holistic therapies, luckily she got out of her paralysed state. She has worked ever since with spirit, helping people all over the world with her clear communication of Past, Present and Future in peoples lives. Communication with loved ones in spirit. Also Tracy Teachers people to develop there sixth sense. She is an Author for her series of Meditation cd's that inspires many people and now is proud to present her first book Inspirational Blessings.

So Tracy has no time for herself but as you can see has well over 27 years of experience, she uses no tools or gimmicks to do her work and works totally natural for the people in the world, she says she's a natural clairvoyant/medium and Author. Also because Tracy wants to help people to develop back the sixth sense they were born with. She has taken qualifications in training TWI. So she become a trainer because some people see titles and can relate to them. When Tracy's mum passed over to spirit she was given a picture of Ernest by an aunty and it was her mums dad.

A Message From The Author

Hi

This is Tracy as I've enjoyed my journey as rough and tumbled has its been, I present this book of Inspirational Blessings to you from the universe. Enjoy and enjoy the message of the day the universe holds for you.

Love and Light

Tracy Poskitt

How to use this book

As you wake up every morning hold your book in your hands, ask the universe for your blessing of the day. Open the book where your eyes meet the page read it .

If you can read it ten times or until you remember it, take it with you throughout your day and know its yours, enjoy.

Blessings

1

The Angels of the universe are holding out there wings of love for you to take from them what you deserve.

2

Love is the ultimate force, but sometimes understanding means more.

Take the understanding of love and have it always.

3

Hold the joy your loved ones in spirit have for you and smile for the rest of the day.

Be the you that you choose to be born as and let the rest of the world enjoy it with love.

5

Be sure that you are unique and allow others to share your gifts because you are special.

6

The universe has all the love we need take what is yours and enjoy being you.

7

You can choose to change the way you look, but your soul shows you as the radiant being you are, people see this and enjoy it so dress your soul and allow others to give you the love and care you deserve.

8

You are now happy you deserve it.

Joy is sent from the energy of the universe to you, take it and have a joyous day.

You are not hurting anyone by having what you want in life, enjoy your wants with love.

11

You are love, you are now attracting loving, satisfying relationships in your life.

12

Everything your heart desires is coming to you easily and without effort now.

13

The radiance of love and light is in you now.

14

The master of the universe is sending you love for your life.

15

You love to love. Today you will be loved.

16

The universe is sending the energy of creation to you in your life.

17

Guidance is sent with love to you for your path of life. Listen to it in your silence.

18

Satisfactory harmony is on its way to you. This will give you a light of all good for you and all around you.

Manifestation is the energy that surrounds you now to create something good or better in your life.

20

Your dynamic, self expression guides joy to all around you.

21

Infinite riches are now flowing freely through you in your life.

22

The blessing of abundance is sent to you now.

23

Thanks, appreciation and love is sent to you from the universe for all you give in life.

24

Divine light and creative energy surrounds you. Allow it to fill your being.

The universe is endlessly beautiful. Just send out a request and every desire in your heart will come to you.

26

There is enough love in the universe for everyone. Take your share today and feel the difference.

27

Everything you hope for from your day is there for the taking. Make sure that you are the one that gets your share. Enjoy the results.

The world is giving you back today some of the beauty and love you have given over the years.

29

You are special. You deserve all the good life offers you.

30

The spiral of prosperity surrounds you.

You are growing in life. So prosper the wish in your heart today.

31

Divine light is working with you. To create miracles in your life.

32

The infinite light is now manifested in your life and all that lives around you.

Today you have been reborn to make your life how you want it to be.

You do not have to hang on to your fears in life. The universal love is here to join you and take care of them.

35

You are lovable and love from all Angels is coming to you here and now.

36

The golden light is given to you for your life to be radiant forever.

37

Love is special and so are you.

38

Your presence of love is required, as you are a person who is recognised.

39

The power of the universe shines through you, Strength and love from all dimensions is sent to you. You give this every day.

Loved ones in spirit are around you healing away the pain in your life with their love.

41

Life seems unfair. Love is sent from the energies above to make it feel better.

42

The abundance of the blessings from the universe come to you from now and forever more.

43

The universe accepts you for who you are with love.

44

You are love, believe this. Look at yourself and enjoy the love that life holds For you.

A ray of love surrounds you. Breath it into your heart and feel the love you deserve.

Peace and Harmony is sent to you from the Angels. Take it for yourself and enjoy it with love.

47

Be happy in your waking hour
and carry this with you all day.
You deserve it.

48

Centuries of life is in your soul. This life is important, live it day by day and endure the love and experience it holds for you.

49

There are whispers of love being sent to you all day. Listen to them and allow love to fulfil you. Feel loved.

50

Your heart is a flower, its pollen is your love. The pollen spreads every day to the people you meet. Your love spreads to all.

51

Your silence is the universes noise. Your thoughts are heard from spirit. They calm them with their love.

52

You are the light for the people in your life. Allow the universal light into your life. You deserve it.

53

A rainbow of healing is surrounding your life, it will make your day better.

54

The Angels are singing there tune to you, listen with love, this is what you deserve.

55

Abundance of life is all around you, so take hold of it with love. Enjoy with all of your being.

56

The sun in the sky shines on you today and always, feel the warmth it has for you.

A material parcel for the universe has been sent to you. It will fulfil your life with wealth.

The coldness that life can be sometimes is warmed up constantly from your heart.

59

You are human Angel that was born, others see this in you. So believe it in yourself.

60

You give your love unconditionally. Allow the universal love to give you some back.

The people in your life appreciate you, believe this and appreciate yourself.

62

Know that your personality is like summertime. It lights up the day and all that is in it.

Feel well as the healing and love surrounds you. Taking away the pain of the day.

64

Your home is the place where you are safe. Take the love that you have put into it, close your door and feel safe and loved.

65

Life is part of the universal energy. Live yours knowing that all the energy you need will guide you to a fulfilled life.

66

Listen to your inner voice, it is telling you how special you are.

67

The vibration of your soul is special and so are you.

68

The animals in spirit surrounds you to give you the unpredictable energy that will uplift your day.

Enjoy your day, the guidance you need is sent to you. Listen to your feelings and follow your heart.

Gold is the ultimate colour,
believe that you are golden to
the people in your life.

71

Allow the flow of the river to take you. Enjoy the messages from the elemental angels of the water. Learn their wisdom to teach you to go with the flow.

72

Look at what you have achieved in your life for the good. Believe that this good has come from you.

Be happy as your soul is charged with the spirit of joy.

74

You are a beautiful being and the universe is proud to be part of you. The people in your life see your beauty everyday.

Radiate your love to all around you. Keep some of the special love for yourself.
It is your birth right.

The colour of your being is showing you how beautiful you are.

77

A heart is beating for you so take the love it holds for you, you deserve it.

78

See the person who you are through the eyes of everyone else, then you will see the joy you are.

You deserve the wisdom that life holds for you, listen to the whispers and the answers to your questions are there for you to hear.

80

The world is full of sunshine allow its rays to shine on you to make your world a brighter place.

81

Breath deeply and feel the person in you that everyone enjoys.

Nature sends you the Angels of love, to fulfil your heart.

83

Feel the freedom that your day holds for you. Be the free spirit who you are.

84

You are full of the joys of life today. As well as sharing it, keep some for yourself.

Prosperity is there in abundance, take your share that is waiting for you.

86

You are living this minute that you worried about a minute ago. So change your thoughts and make it a better one.

Your body is a temple and stands perfect for all to see, enjoy it with love and admiration like everyone else dose.

The rainbow in the sky is there for you, take your special colour and allow it to radiate your day.

89

Know you are loved, believe it and listen to the heart beat of the universe.

90

Take the healing that you need. You deserve to feel better.

You are the inspiration what your family needs, you are special.

92

The catalogue of the universe is yours so go shopping for all your heart desires.

93

Allow the wings of the Angels to wrap you up with the healing and love you need in your life it is special.

When you feel alone listen to your heart and let it give you the love that you give to everyone else.

95

You are special, the world would not be without you so allow the world to give you the special gifts it holds for you in your life.

96

All what you need will be sent to you. Take it with both hands and make your day a better one.

97

Your brightness lights up your life and all who is in it.

The maker made a special soul when you was born.

99

The healing ray shines on you to take away the pain and suffering in your life.

Food of life is feeding you with all of the nourishment you deserve.

101

There's seven day in this week, you deserve today as its special for you.

102

You are magnetic everyone wants your energy as its pure love.

Take your share of money, love and happiness that you deserve, if you don't someone else will be there to take it.

104

Breath in love and hold what is rightfully yours, it's the universe giving back to you the love you share every second of every day.

The natural energy of healing flows through, this is passed on from you every time you speak to somebody.

Take the smiles out of the day, you deserve to be happy.

107

Know that you've been sent by the universe, sing the special song of your life, enjoy the harmony that's there for you.

108

Just be you today because this is who everyone enjoys.

109

Everyone you touch receives a special gift as you are special.

110

Know that the people in your life, send gratitude to you for all that you are and do.

Conclusion

I hope that this book has been guided to you for all the reasons that you deserve.

Enjoy its inspiration and know that Tracy Poskitt is just the author. It is the love that has been passed through her as a channel from spirit that gives you this gift of inspiration with love and light.

I hope that your heart has been uplifted and inspired by the love that these blessings present to you. Tracy would like to show her gratitude by thanking you. Tracy's work also involves one to one consultations of messages from spirit covering past, present and future in your life and communication from your personal loved ones in spirit. Tracy also is doing many shows internationally demonstrating her work and has done so over her twenty seven years of experience.

For more information, dates, venues contact Guidelines International

07756583404

www.GuidelinesInternational.com

Thanks Tracy Poskitt

Lightning Source UK Ltd.
Milton Keynes UK
27 January 2011

166492UK00001B/4/P

9 781426 951855